# NORTH DAKOTA

BY LYNN TERNUS

CONTENT CONSULTANT
Kimberly K. Porter, PhD
Department of History
University of North Dakota

Core Library

An Imprint of Abdo Publishing
abdobooks.com

abdobooks.com

Published by Abdo Publishing, a division of ABDO, PO Box 398166, Minneapolis, Minnesota 55439.


Printed in the United States of America, North Mankato, Minnesota.
052022
092022

Cover Photo: Shutterstock Images
Interior Photos: Shutterstock Images, 4–5, 17 (flower), 18, 23, 26–27, 29, 30; Jacob Boomsma/Shutterstock Images, 7, 43; Red Line Editorial, 9 (North Dakota), 9 (USA); Danita Delimont Photography/Newscom, 10–11; Brian Baer/Sacramento Bee/Tribune News Service/Getty Images, 13; iStockphoto, 17 (flag); David Spates/Shutterstock Images, 17 (bird); Martin Prochazkacz/Shutterstock Images, 17 (fish); Amelia Martin/Shutterstock Images, 17 (fruit); Randall Runtsch/Shutterstock Images, 20–21, 45; Mike Ehrmann/Getty Images Sport/Getty Images, 34–35; Paul Schmidt/iStockphoto, 39; Roy K. Miller/Icon Sportswire/AP Images, 40

Editor: Marie Pearson
Series Designer: Joshua Olson

**Library of Congress Control Number: 2021951397**

**Publisher's Cataloging-in-Publication Data**

Names: Ternus, Lynn, author.
Title: North Dakota / by Lynn Ternus
Description: Minneapolis, Minnesota : Abdo Publishing, 2023 | Series: Core library of US states | Includes online resources and index.
Identifiers: ISBN 9781532197758 (lib. bdg.) | ISBN 9781098270513 (ebook)
Subjects: LCSH: U.S. states--Juvenile literature. | Midwest States--Juvenile literature. | North Dakota--History--Juvenile literature. | Physical geography--United States--Juvenile literature.
Classification: DDC 978.4--dc23

Population demographics broken down by race and ethnicity come from the 2019 census estimate. Population totals come from the 2020 census.

# CONTENTS

CHAPTER ONE

# THE PEACE GARDEN STATE

Visitors walk along paved paths at the International Peace Garden. In the garden, ponds reflect the clear sky. Birds chirp in the trees. Colorful flowers bloom. Workers trim bushes and shrubs. The garden is on both sides of the border of North Dakota and Manitoba, Canada. It's a symbol of the peaceful relationship between the United States and Canada. It gives North Dakota its nickname, the Peace Garden State.

A channel at the International Peace Garden marks the US-Canadian border.

## BUILDING THE GARDEN

In 1929 the National Association of Gardeners gave the green light for the International Peace Garden to be built. The group wanted the garden to be near the center of North America, so it was built in Dunseith, North Dakota, and Boissevain, Manitoba. North Dakota gave 888 acres (359 ha) of land to the project, and Manitoba gave 1,451 acres (587 ha). Around 50,000 people from both countries came to watch the dedication and groundbreaking ceremony in 1932.

## ABOUT NORTH DAKOTA

North Dakota is part of the Midwest region of the United States. Canada borders the state's northern side. Minnesota lies to the east. South Dakota is to the south, and Montana is to the west.

Grand Forks and Fargo are two of North Dakota's largest cities. Both were built along the Red River on the state's eastern border. These cities have the two biggest colleges in the state. North Dakota State University is in Fargo. The University of North Dakota is in Grand Forks. North Dakota's

Grand Forks lies on the Red River.

capital, Bismarck, is in the middle of the state. It is on the Missouri River.

The Midwest is known for its flat farm fields. North Dakota has wide-open prairies. Farmers grow crops that are shipped all over the United States and beyond. In the northeastern part of the state, anglers and boaters enjoy Devils Lake. Devils Lake is the largest

## PERSPECTIVES

### HIGH QUALITY OF LIFE

**In 2018 *US News & World Report* did a US quality of life ranking, and North Dakota ranked number one. The report found that the state's rural, small towns give people a positive social environment. In North Dakota, people often show support for their neighbors. They also engage in community service and feel like they're making a big difference. North Dakota's natural environment, including great air quality, also helped it rank high on the quality-of-life list. North Dakota governor Doug Burgum said about the state, "I think something truly special about North Dakota is the way people are invested in it and how they love the state and they love their communities."**

natural lake in North Dakota. People fish for walleye, pike, and perch there all year long. In the western part of the state, hikers walk among petrified trees. The mighty Missouri River flows across much of North Dakota. Oil, gas, and wind companies in the state supply electricity for the nation. There is much to see and learn in North Dakota.

# MAP OF NORTH DAKOTA

**North Dakota has many important locations. How do the locations on the map help you better understand Chapter One?**

CHAPTER TWO

# HISTORY OF NORTH DAKOTA

People have been living in the area that is now North Dakota for approximately 10,000 years. Scientists believe the first people came to this area after the last ice age. People living there hunted large animals. Some eventually settled into a farming lifestyle.

Several American Indian nations lived near the Missouri River. The Mandan, Hidatsa, and Sahnish (Arikara) were three of the largest. Scientists believe the Mandan settled the area

Mandan, Hidatsa, and Sahnish people continue to teach their children and visitors about their historic ways of life at Fort Berthold Indian Reservation.

around 900 CE. The Hidatsa and Sahnish peoples came later. Hidatsa and Mandan people likely migrated from what is now Minnesota. Sahnish people came from present-day Iowa and Kansas. All three of these nations used the river for transportation. They relied on bison herds for food, clothes, shelter, and tools. They also farmed. Most of these peoples stayed in one village all year long. People from these three nations continue to live in North Dakota today.

## COLONIZING THE AREA

In the mid-1700s, Europeans came into the region. At this time, the Hidatsa, Mandan, and Sahnish peoples were living on the Missouri River. The Ojibwe and Cree lived in the northeastern region. And the northern, western, and southeastern areas were home to Nakota, Lakota, and Dakota peoples. Some white people wanted to trade goods with these nations. In 1801 they built a trading post on the Red River at present-day Pembina. American Indians traded furs and meat for metal tools, guns, cloth, and other goods. However,

Today people of the Standing Rock Sioux Tribe belong to the Lakota and Dakota nations. David Gipp was among those who worked to promote the tribe's interests in the 2000s.

these dealings had risks. Europeans brought diseases to North America and infected American Indian people. In the 1800s smallpox killed many American Indians.

In 1803 the US government purchased a large area of land west of the Mississippi River from France. This was called the Louisiana Purchase. President Thomas Jefferson asked a group to explore the region. Meriwether Lewis and William Clark led the group. They reached what is now North Dakota in 1804.

## PERSPECTIVES

### SACAGAWEA

**Sacagawea was Shoshone by birth. When she was a teenager, Hidatsa people raided her village and took her captive. The Hidatsa then adopted her into their culture. Sacagawea married French Canadian trader Toussaint Charbonneau. The two joined the Lewis and Clark expedition. Sacagawea helped translate between the expedition and Shoshone and Hidatsa people. She helped them find food, and she provided many other important services. Clark said of her aid, "[She deserved] a greater reward for her attention and services on that rout[e] than we had in our power to give her."**

Several American Indian nations, such as the Hidatsa and Mandan peoples, helped them during their first winter.

Relations between American Indian nations and European traders were mostly peaceful at first. But by the mid-1800s, the arrival of more white people began changing the ways of life of American Indians. A railroad allowed white people to travel easily to and through the area in the 1870s. White people killed thousands of bison in the late 1800s. When American Indian people tried to defend their lands, the US Army built military forts to fight them.

## FARMING AND INDUSTRY

In the 1870s, even more white settlers streamed into the territory. More than 100,000 people arrived between 1879 and 1886. Many created huge farms. Some others worked in the new lignite mines in the west. Lignite is a type of coal that is used for fuel. The US government forced American Indians onto reservations. If nations tried to stay on their lands, the US Army pushed them out.

North and South Dakota became states on the same day in 1889. No one knows which state's paper the president signed first. But North Dakota is called the thirty-ninth state and South Dakota the fortieth. During the first half of the 1900s, industries changed in the state. Machines made farming more efficient.

## STATEHOOD

The road to statehood for North and South Dakota wasn't always smooth. In 1861 these areas were part of the Dakota Territory. But the northern and southern regions didn't always get along well. The south had a much larger population. People there viewed the northern area as a wild, lawless place. In the 1880s the southern region had enough people to form a state. It wanted to break away from the north. But the federal government refused at first. It said the area could either be one big state or the south would have to wait until the north got enough people to qualify for statehood. The north eventually reached the required 60,000 people. On November 2, 1889, North Dakota and South Dakota became separate states.

People began building dams to produce hydroelectricity. But the dams also flooded American Indian lands. Then, in the 1970s, one of North Dakota's first oil booms occurred. The oil boom changed North Dakota's economy. Oil continues to be an important part of North Dakota's economy into the 2020s.

## GOVERNMENT

Today North Dakota's state government has three branches. The legislative branch is

# NORTH DAKOTA
# QUICK FACTS

**There is a lot that makes North Dakota special. Why do you think these facts and symbols are special for North Dakotans?**

**Abbreviation:** ND
**Nickname:** The Peace Garden State
**Motto:** Liberty and union now and forever, one and inseparable
**Date of statehood:** November 2, 1889
**Capital:** Bismarck
**Population:** 779,094
**Area:** 70,698 square miles (183,107 sq km)

## STATE SYMBOLS

**State bird**
Western meadowlark

**State flower**
Wild prairie rose

**State fish**
Northern pike

**State fruit**
Chokecherry

A hydroelectric dam on Lake Sakakawea generates electricity in North Dakota.

divided into the Senate and House of Representatives. Elected officials in the legislative branch write, change, and vote on new bills. Bills that pass in the legislative branch go on to the executive branch. The governor leads this branch and can choose to sign bills into law. The judicial branch consists of the courts. The highest court in the state is the North Dakota Supreme Court.

North Dakota also has five federally recognized tribes. These tribes are the Mandan, Hidatsa, and Arikara Nation; the Sisseton-Wahpeton Oyate Nation; the Spirit Lake Nation; the Standing Rock Sioux Tribe; and the Turtle Mountain Band of Chippewa Indians. Each of these tribes has its own system of government.

# STRAIGHT TO THE SOURCE

The North Dakota region experienced a population boom in the late 1800s and early 1900s. People from many ethnic backgrounds came to the area. Larry Remele of the State Historical Society of North Dakota noted:

> *Many were immigrants of Scandinavian or Germanic origin. Norwegians were the largest single ethnic group. . . . A small, but strong community of Scotch-Irish-English background played an especially influential role, contributing many of North Dakota's early business and political leaders. Many other groups, including Asians, Blacks, and Arabs, settled throughout North Dakota. So significant was this foreign immigration that in 1915 over 79% of all North Dakotans were either immigrants or children of immigrants.*

Source: Larry Remele. "Summary of North Dakota History—American Settlement." *State Historical Society of North Dakota*, 2021, history.nd.gov. Accessed 4 May 2021.

## BACK IT UP

The author of this passage is using evidence to support a point. Write a paragraph describing the point the author is making. Then write down two or three pieces of evidence the author uses to support his point.

CHAPTER THREE

# GEOGRAPHY AND CLIMATE

North Dakota has three main regions. Each region has different features and landforms. These regions are the Red River Valley, the Drift Prairie, and the Missouri Plateau.

The valley and prairie regions formed during the glacial periods. Between 2.6 million and 11,700 years ago, huge slabs of ice and snow covered large parts of North America. This included present-day North Dakota. The Red River Valley in the east is what remains of

Many people enjoy seeing the beauty of the Badlands.

a glacial lake. Thousands of years ago, a glacier melted and formed a lake. The lake dried up, but the valley and its rich soil remains. The Drift Prairie is also in the east. As glaciers receded, sediments remained in the area, forming the soil. The Drift Prairie is mostly flat but also has some hills.

The Missouri Plateau in the west is part of the Great Plains. Glaciers did not cover this area during the last ice age. The plateau has rolling hills and several rivers. This area also contains the Badlands. The rocky canyons of the Badlands began

## PERSPECTIVES

### THE BADLANDS

**The Badlands gets its name from the Lakota. They called the area *mako sica*, which was translated to "bad lands." European explorers also said the region was "bad lands to travel across." Today many people visit the Badlands to see its natural beauty. The landscape stretches into South Dakota. Travel blogger Joe Baur was stunned when he traveled to the Badlands for the first time. He said, "It really was one of the most beautiful sights I'd ever seen."**

The Drift Prairie has many small potholes, which are pools of water that dry up seasonally.

forming approximately 65 million years ago. At this time, shallow seas covered the area. Sand, silt, mud, and clay piled on top of one another. Later, volcanic ash also created layers. Over millions of years, water slowly wore away some of the sediment. Rivers, snow, ice, rain, and wind helped erode parts of the layers. Hills and valleys formed, creating the rugged, colorful Badlands people recognize today. Another feature often found in the Badlands is petrified wood. These logs, trees, and stumps fossilized over millions of years.

North Dakota has several state and national parks. Bison roam in Theodore Roosevelt National Park in western North Dakota. Part of this park includes the Badlands. Fort Abraham Lincoln State Park was created in 1907. It is the oldest state park in North Dakota. There, visitors learn about frontier history in the area.

## AMERICAN BISON

**The bison is one of the most famous animals on the Great Plains. Bison are the largest mammals in North America. Males weigh as much as 2,000 pounds (900 kg). The animals have thick, woolly fur that keeps them warm during winter. They live in herds led by older female bison. Male bison stay around a herd during breeding season, which takes place in the summer. Once breeding season ends, males leave the herd. They form small groups or set off on their own.**

## CLIMATE AND WILDLIFE

North Dakota has hot summers and cold winters. The Rocky Mountains block humid air from the Pacific Ocean. So winters tend to be cold and dry. The state is often windy.

Its flat prairies have few trees to block the winds. During winter, powerful winds increase the likelihood of blizzards.

Weather and landforms affect what plants and animals live in the state. Many grasses grow in the prairies. Elk and other grazing animals rely on these habitats. Badgers and prairie skinks also live in these grasslands. Prairie skinks are small reptiles that hide under flat rocks. Prairie dogs and mountain lions are common in the western part of the state.

## EXPLORE ONLINE

**Chapter Three discusses Theodore Roosevelt National Park. As you know, every source is different. The website below has more information about the park. How is the information from the website the same as the information in Chapter Three? What new information did you learn from the website?**

### GEOLOGIC FORMATIONS

**abdocorelibrary.com/north-dakota**

CHAPTER FOUR

# RESOURCES AND ECONOMY

North Dakota has many natural resources. For this reason, most of North Dakota's economy depends on the land. Agriculture and energy production are some of the state's biggest industries.

North Dakota's rich soil is good for crops. In the past, thousands of people moved to the area to farm. In 1870 the area had around 1,720 farms. Each was an average of 176 acres (71 ha). By 1890, about 27,611 farms were in North Dakota. These farms were

Some North Dakota ranchers raise cattle.

## PERSPECTIVES

### FARMING THE LAND

**Joe Morken's family has farmed in North Dakota for generations. Morken works 3,400 acres (1,375 ha) of land near Casselton. He grows corn, soybeans, and sugar beets. Morken notes that the weather, especially winter, can be harsh in North Dakota. Farmers have no time to waste. "Our window is so short for harvest, and you have to go nuts until you get everything off. . . . We have to get the crops up and have the field dug before it freezes solid," he said. But Morken loves his land, noting, "This valley, the soil that was created and left behind, boy, I find it hard to believe there's any dirt better than right here."**

277 acres (112 ha) on average. In the 1930s the number of family-run ranches and farms decreased. But the farms that remained grew larger. This change was due to several factors, including new technology that helped people farm more efficiently.

Today almost 90 percent of the land in North Dakota is used for farming and ranching. The state is a leading producer of wheat, rye, and

Wind turbines across North Dakota generate energy from the blowing wind, which turns the blades of the turbines.

sugar beets. These crops are sold throughout the nation and the world. North Dakotans also raise livestock such as cattle, pigs, chickens, and bison.

## ENERGY INDUSTRY

Energy is the biggest industry in North Dakota. The state creates six times more energy than it uses. The state's strong winds power huge wind turbines.

From 2016 to 2017, people gathered at the Oceti Sakowin Camp in North Dakota to protest the building of the Dakota Access Pipeline.

Wind farms create 25 percent of the state's electricity. The rest of the energy comes from fossil fuels such as coal, oil, and natural gas. Fossil fuels formed over millions of years from the remains of dead plants and animals.

In 2002 technology advanced enough to drill for oil deep in the northwest corner of the state. By 2006 small towns in the area doubled in size. People came from around the country to work in the oil fields. The oil boom helped many towns financially. However, the oil industry also has some negative aspects. Oil drilling destroys wildlife habitats. Most oil is transported through pipelines that crisscross the country. Sometimes the pipelines leak. This can hurt the environment.

North Dakota has 16 major oil pipelines and nine major natural gas pipelines. In total the state's pipelines

## THE DAKOTA ACCESS PIPELINE

The Dakota Access Pipeline stretches from North Dakota to Illinois. Part of the pipeline runs less than 1 mile (1.6 km) from the Standing Rock Sioux Tribe's reservation. People from the tribe protested the pipeline's construction in 2016. The tribe said that if the pipeline spilled and polluted the Missouri River, it would hurt their access to clean drinking water. But the US government let the pipeline be built. It moves oil from North Dakota to the Midwest and south to the Gulf Coast. In 2021 the pipeline was scheduled to undergo an environmental review.

stretch approximately 30,000 miles (48,000 km) through the state. In 2020 North Dakota was the second-largest state in oil production. North Dakota often produces around 1 million barrels of oil each day.

North Dakotans also still mine lignite. The state has five mines that extract 30 million tons (27 million metric tons) of this product each year. It's the state's main source of fuel for electricity. Almost 20 percent of the world's lignite is in North Dakota.

## OTHER INDUSTRIES

North Dakota's other natural resources include gravel, sand, cement rock, salt, uranium, and clay. Some of these resources, including gravel and sand, are used for construction work, such as making concrete. Uranium is used as fuel for nuclear power plants.

North Dakotans also work in service industries. These include travel, transportation, and finance companies. Thousands of people work at US Air Force bases in Grand Forks and Minot.

# STRAIGHT TO THE SOURCE

North Dakota's industries are tied tightly to its natural resources. The state government notes:

> *The North Dakota landscape is rich in beauty, but it's also a treasure trove of natural resources that are fueling our state in more ways than one. Oil and lignite coal. Natural gas and biofuels. Wind and solar. North Dakota's energy industry supports more than 75,000 direct and indirect jobs and accounts for more than $3.2 billion annually and offers some of the most significant growth opportunities for our state.*

Source: "Energy & Natural Resources." *North Dakota*, 2020, nd.gov. Accessed 4 May 2021.

## WHAT'S THE BIG IDEA?

Take a close look at this passage. What is the main connection being made between North Dakota and its resources? Explain how the main idea is supported by details, naming two or three of these supporting details.

USA
USA

# PEOPLE AND PLACES

North Dakota boasts a number of famous people. Monique Lamoureux-Morando and Jocelyne Lamoureux-Davidson are twin sisters. They were born in Grand Forks. They played on the US women's national hockey team and in the Olympics. In 2018 they were part of Team USA, competing for the Olympic gold medal in hockey. The team was playing Canada, its biggest rival. The US women's hockey team hadn't won an Olympic gold for 20 years,

**Monique Lamoureux-Morando, *left*, and Jocelyne Lamoureux-Davidson, *right*, played hockey for the University of North Dakota in college.**

but the twins helped change that. Their goals brought the team to victory. Other famous people from North Dakota include musician Gwen Sebastian, actor Kellan Lutz, football player Jim Kleinsasser, and actor Josh Duhamel. Author Louise Erdrich grew up in the state.

An estimated 779,094 people live in North Dakota. The state is mostly rural, but approximately half of its people live in cities. Fargo is the largest city, with approximately 125,990 people. Bismarck is the second largest, with

## PERSPECTIVES

### BISMARCK CHURCHILLS

**In the early 1900s, professional baseball was segregated. Black athletes were not allowed to play with white athletes. But that was not true for some semiprofessional leagues. In North Dakota, the Bismarck Churchills had an integrated team. Black and white athletes played together. Satchel Paige was one of the Black players on the team. He is considered one of the best pitchers of all time. The Bismarck Churchills were so good that even professional teams played against them.**

a population of more than 73,000. Other larger cities include Grand Forks and Minot.

Approximately 84 percent of the state's population is white people who are not Hispanic or Latino. The next largest demographic group is American Indians at 5.6 percent. Hispanic or Latino people make up 4.1 percent of the population, and Black people make up 3.4 percent of people. According to the North Dakota Census Office,

## HISTORIC SITES

**North Dakota boasts many sites where visitors can learn about the state's rich history. The North Dakota Heritage Center and State Museum in Bismarck covers it all. It provides information about what the area was like 600 million years ago and examines history up to the present time. Jamestown boasts the oldest standing courthouse in the state. The building is known for its unique architecture. At Fort Mandan in Washburn, visitors can see the reconstructed fort where Lewis and Clark lived during their journey through the state. In Stanton visitors to the Knife River Indian Villages National Historic Site learn how the area's American Indian peoples once lived.**

the Chippewa, Dakota, and Lakota peoples make up approximately 72 percent of the American Indian population in the state. Most live on one of the state's five reservations.

Various American Indian peoples come together in Bismarck to hold a cultural celebration each September. It's called the United Tribes Technical College International Powwow. It features competitive dancing. Participants and visitors can experience the rich histories of many nations.

## ENTERTAINMENT AND ACTIVITIES

The state's large open areas are perfect for outdoor sports and recreation. People often bike when the weather is nice. Some enjoy biking the Maah Daah Hey Trail in Theodore Roosevelt National Park. People also go kayaking and hiking. Some camp in the state and national parks. During the winter, hockey is a popular sport at both indoor and outdoor rinks.

**The Maah Daah Hey Trail is very long and can be challenging in parts.**

Brock Boeser is one of many National Hockey League stars who played for the University of North Dakota in college.

North Dakota doesn't have any major professional sports teams. But people in the state are passionate about supporting their local high school and college teams. They cheer on the Fighting Hawks hockey team at the University of North Dakota. This team is known for its eight national championships between 1959 and 2016. North Dakota State University has a successful football team. By 2019 the team had eight Football

Championship Subdivision national championships. That was more than any other team. Many North Dakotans take pride in their local athletic teams. Whether people are spending time on the trail, in the city, in the rink, or watching games, North Dakota has something for everyone.

## FURTHER EVIDENCE

**Chapter Five discusses North Dakota's sports teams. What was one of the main points of this chapter? What evidence is included to support this point? Read the article at the website below. Does the information on the website support the main point of the chapter? Does it present new evidence?**

### BUILDING COMMUNITIES: SPORTS

**abdocorelibrary.com/north-dakota**

# IMPORTANT DATES

**10,000 years ago**

People begin living in the region that eventually becomes North Dakota.

**900 CE**

The Mandan people move near the Missouri River.

**1700s**

Europeans start trading with American Indian peoples.

**1803**

The US government purchases a large area of land from France that includes present-day North Dakota.

**1889**

North Dakota becomes the thirty-ninth state on November 2.

**1932**

The groundbreaking ceremony for the International Peace Garden is held.

**2016**
The Standing Rock Sioux protest the construction of an oil pipeline near their reservation.

**2020**
North Dakota is the second-largest producer of oil in the United States.

# STOP AND THINK

## Say What?

Studying US states and history can mean learning a lot of new vocabulary. Find five words in this book you've never heard before. Use a dictionary to find out what they mean. Then write the meanings in your own words and use each word in a new sentence.

## Take a Stand

North Dakota is mostly rural. Much of the state has wide-open spaces. Half of the people live in rural areas, while half live in cities. Do you think one of these places is better to live in than the other? Why or why not?

## You Are There

This book discusses the three main regions in North Dakota. Imagine you are traveling through each one. Write a letter home telling your friends about the experience. What plants and animals do you see? What does the climate feel like? Be sure to add plenty of detail to your notes.

## Another View

This book talks about fossil fuels. As you know, every source is different. Ask a librarian or another adult to help you find another source about this topic. Write a short essay comparing and contrasting the new source's point of view with that of this book's author. What is the point of view of each author? How are they similar and why? How are they different and why?

# GLOSSARY

**boom**
a sudden, large increase in growth

**erode**
to wear away by the movement of wind, water, or other natural forces

**federal**
having to do with the national government

**glacial**
having to do with large bodies of ice that move slowly across land

**habitat**
the place where a plant or an animal lives

**humid**
having a lot of moisture in the air

**petrified**
turned to stone

**rural**
having to do with the countryside

**sediment**
small bits of material that settle at the bottom of a body of water or are carried away by water or wind

**segregate**
to separate groups of people based on race, class, or ethnicity

# ONLINE RESOURCES

To learn more about North Dakota, visit our free resource websites below.

Visit **abdocorelibrary.com** or scan this QR code for free Common Core resources for teachers and students, including vetted activities, multimedia, and booklinks, for deeper subject comprehension.

Visit **abdobooklinks.com** or scan this QR code for free additional online weblinks for further learning. These links are routinely monitored and updated to provide the most current information available.

# LEARN MORE

Gagne, Tammy. *Exploring the Midwest*. Abdo, 2018.

Hewson, Anthony K. *US Women's Hockey Team*. Abdo, 2019.

Powell, Marie. *Traditional Stories of the Plains Nations*. Abdo, 2018.

## About the Author

Lynn Ternus is a children's book writer who lives in northern Minnesota.